PIANO VOCAL GUITAR

COUNTRY STRONG

MUSIC FROM THE MOTION PICTURE SOUNDTRACK

T0077126

ISBN 978-1-4584-0085-7

HAL•LEONARD®
CORPORATION
7777 W. BLUEMOUND RD. P.O. BOX 13819 MILWAUKEE, WI 53213

Visit Hal Leonard Online at
www.halleonard.com